Ten of the Best: Stories of Exploration and Adventure

TEN OF THE BEST ADVENTURES IN

NEW WORLDS

Crabtree Publishing Company
www.crabtreebooks.com

Crabtree Publishing Company

www.crabtreebooks.com

1-800-387-7650

Publishing in Canada
616 Welland Ave.
St. Catharines, ON
L2M 5V6

Published in the United States
PMB 59051, 350 Fifth Ave.
59th Floor,
New York, NY

Published in **2016 by CRABTREE PUBLISHING COMPANY.**

Printed in Canada/082015/BF20150630

Project development, design, and concept:
   David West Children's Books

Author and designer: David West

Illustrator: David West

Contributing editor: Steve Parker

Editor: Kathy Middleton

Proofreader: Rebecca Sjonger

**Production coordinator
   and Prepress technician**: Ken Wright

Print coordinator: Margaret Amy Salter

Library and Archives Canada Cataloguing in Publication

West, David, 1956-, author
      Ten of the best adventures in new worlds / David West.

(Ten of the best : stories of exploration and adventure)
Includes index.
Issued in print and electronic formats.
ISBN 978-0-7787-1835-2 (bound).--
ISBN 978-0-7787-1841-3 (paperback).--
ISBN 978-1-4271-7803-9 (pdf).--ISBN 978-1-4271-7797-1 (html)

      1. Discoveries in geography--Juvenile literature. 2. Explorers--
Juvenile
literature. I. Title. II. Title: Adventures in new worlds.

G175.W47 2015   j910.9   C2015-903038-2
                                                 C2015-903039-0

Library of Congress Cataloging-in-Publication Data

CIP available at the Library of Congress

CONTENTS

The Prisoner's Tale 4

La Noche Triste 6

Battle of Punta Quemada 8

Fighting the Iroquois 10

Mutiny 12

Grizzly Attack! 14

Lion Attack! 16

The Berbera Disaster 18

Nine Hours Too Late 20

Lost in the Desert 22

Glossary and Index 24

4

The Prisoner's Tale

Around 1298, Italian writer Rustichello da Pisa was being held prisoner in a jail in Genoa. At one point, he was joined by a prisoner from Venice, a rich merchant captured in a sea battle. Rustichello wrote down the merchant's life story. It was published as *The Travels of Marco Polo*.

Marco Polo

Marco Polo first met his father in 1269. Marco was 17. His father, Niccolò, and uncle, Maffeo, were traveling merchants who had been away for many years. In 1271, Marco joined them on their voyage to fulfill a request made by the emperor of China, Kublai Khan. The emperor had asked them to bring him oil from the lamp from the tomb of Jesus Christ in Jerusalem. After fetching the oil, they rode camels to the port of Hormuz in Persia. The ships did not seem seaworthy, so they carried on by land. They reached the emperor's palace in Shangdu three and a half years later.

Marco knew four languages and had acquired knowledge useful to Kublai Khan. He became a government official in China and made many visits to China's southern and eastern provinces. After 18 years of service, the Polos wanted to leave, but Kublai Khan did not want to let them go. In 1292, he did allow them to accompany a young Chinese bride to her wedding to the ruler of Persia—Kublai Khan's great nephew.

They left China on a fleet of 14 ships. The journey took two years—as well as the lives of 600 travelers. Only 18 survived. Upon learning of Kublai Khan's death, the Polos headed home to Venice.

Although Marco Polo was not the first European to visit China, he was the first to write about what he saw there. His writings inspired many explorers and adventurers, including Christopher Columbus.

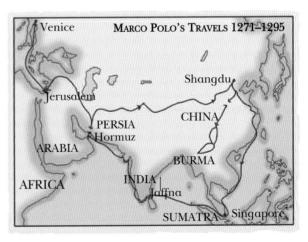

La Noche Triste

Hernán Cortés

During the Spanish conquest of central America from 1519 to 1521, a soldier and fortune hunter named Hernán Cortés captured the Aztec emperor, Moctezuma, in the capital city, Tenochtitlan. Cortés had achieved this with an army of 600 **conquistadors** and native warriors from the Tlaxcala people. In 1520, Cortés returned to Tenochtitlan from an expedition to find that his second in command had massacred many of the Aztec nobles. The people of the city rebelled against the invading Spaniards as well as Moctezuma. They killed Moctezuma when he tried to speak to them, then attacked the Spanish soldiers and their native allies.

Under constant attack, and with gunpowder, food, and water in short supply, Cortés realized that they would have to leave the city. He made plans to escape at night across Lake Texcoco, along one of the many **causeways** that linked the city to the lake's shore. Wagons and horses were loaded with Aztec treasure, and Cortés encouraged his soldiers to carry as much gold as they could. Under the cover of a rainstorm, the large army headed for the Tacuba causeway, but they were discovered before they got out of the city. As they reached the causeway, hundreds of canoes carrying Aztec warriors appeared. Firing arrows and launching attacks with **obsidian**-bladed weapons, they attacked the fleeing army. Many of the soldiers lost their footing and fell into the lake. Weighed down by gold and equipment they drowned. Cortés charged ahead but only half his army followed. The rest died in the lake or were killed by Aztecs during *La Noche Triste*—The Night of Sorrow.

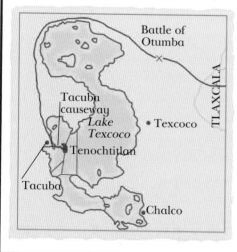

Two weeks later, Cortés held off an Aztec army at the Battle of Otumba. This gave the Spaniards and their allies an advantage, and they reached the safety of the city of Tlaxcala. A year later, Cortés returned to Tenochtitlan with a huge army. He took the city on August 13, 1521, marking the end of the Aztec empire.

Battle of Punta Quemada

In November 1524, Spanish conquistador Francisco Pizarro, a distant cousin of explorer Hernán Cortés, left Panama and headed for Peru with about 80 men to find the Inca tribe and their gold. By January 1525, his small band had reached an abandoned village in Colombia. Many of his men had died along the way from starvation and illness.

Francisco Pizarro

Pizarro sent Lieutenant Montenegro back to Panama with some men to get supplies while the rest of the troops secured the village against attack. Emerging from the jungle, Montenegro's troops were ambushed by the local Quitians. Under a barrage of flying arrows, Montenegro rallied his men and charged at the native people who fled in terror. Fearing that Pizarro might be attacked next, Montenegro immediately started back to the village.

Another group of Quitians, however, had tried to take their village back from Pizarro at the same time as the first ambush. Pizarro, who had a fiery temper, led his men in a charge against them. The native warriors counterattacked. Just when it seemed as though the Spaniards would be overwhelmed, Montenegro and his men arrived, attacking the Quitians from the rear. The warriors fled back to the jungle. Pizarro survived but suffered seven separate wounds.

Pizarro chose to end his expedition and returned to Panama. After a second attempt to conquer the Incas failed in 1528, Pizarro set out once again in 1532. He eventually captured the Inca ruler Atahualpa and defeated 50,000 Inca warriors with a force of just 150 men at the Battle of Cajamarca on November 16, 1532.

Fighting the Iroquois

Samuel de Champlain

Born in 1574, explorer Samuel de Champlain began his exploration of North America in 1603 on behalf of France. He established the city of Quebec in the northern **colony** called New France, now part of Canada. He also explored and mapped the Atlantic coast and the Great Lakes. Champlain wrote a book about his journeys.

In the summer of 1609, Champlain began to establish friendly relationships with the local native people. He made **alliances** with the Wendat (called Huron by the French), the Algonquian, and other tribes living near the St. Lawrence River. Champlain agreed to help the native people in their longstanding war against the Iroquois, another native group that lived farther south.

Champlain set off to explore the Richelieu River with nine French soldiers and 300 native people. On this journey, he discovered and mapped a lake, which he named after himself. They had not come across any Iroquois so many of the men headed back, leaving Champlain with two French soldier and 60 native people. Only a few days later, they came upon a large group of Iroquois, south of Lake Champlain.

As the native warriors attacked Champlain's smaller force, he fired at the Iroquois chiefs—killing two with a single shot from his **arquebus**. The third chief was killed by one of the French soldiers. The rest of the Iroquois fled, chased by the victorious Algonquian warriors.

This led to a century of bad relations between French settlers and the Iroquois people. In 1615, Champlain set off on an expedition farther into uncharted parts of New France accompanied by ten French soldiers and 300 Huron warriors. While attacking a well-defended Iroquois village, Champlain was lucky to escape with his life. Wounded twice in the leg by arrows, he was forced to flee with the Huron and spend the winter with them. At one point, Champlain got lost while on a deer hunt and spent three days living off the land. He was finally able to return to the settlement at Quebec the following year.

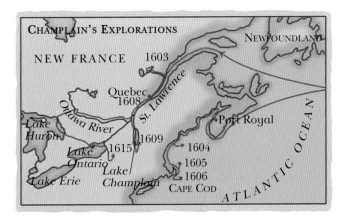

CHAMPLAIN'S EXPLORATIONS

NEW FRANCE   1603   NEWFOUNDLAND

Quebec
1608   St. Lawrence
Lake   Ottawa River   Port Royal
Huron
1609   1604
Lake   1615   1605
Ontario   Lake   1606
Lake Erie   Champlain   CAPE COD

ATLANTIC OCEAN

Champlain led many more expeditions as well as returning to France, making no less than 25 return trips across the Atlantic in his lifetime, without losing a single ship. In 1633, he was made lieutenant general of New France and died there two years later.

Mutiny

René-Robert Cavelier, Sieur de La Salle

Born into a noble family in France, Robert de La Salle studied to be a priest. But by the age of 22, he knew he wanted a more adventurous life. In 1666, he set out for New France to seek his fortune. His arrogant and demanding attitude seemed to inspire loyalty and confidence in many of his men during his expeditions in the **New World**.

After returning home, La Salle received a title of nobility from the king of France in 1677, as well as permission to explore the borders of New France. A year later he returned to the New World with Henri de Tonti, an Italian **soldier of fortune**. After many setbacks, La Salle fulfilled his ambition to travel down the Mississippi River.

On April 9, 1682, La Salle and Tonti arrived at the mouth of the great river. They claimed all the land in the Mississippi **basin** for France and named the region Louisiana for King Louis XIV.

La Salle convinced the king to allow him to set up a colony in Louisiana. In 1684, La Salle left for the New World once again, this time with a large expedition and a plan to establish a French colony at the mouth of the Mississippi. They had four ships and 300 colonists, but they would not

reach their destination. An error in navigation sent the ships to Matagorda Bay—500 miles (805 km) west of where they intended to land. In addition, one ship was lost to pirates, one was wrecked, and a third returned to France.

After just a few months, more than half of the settlers in the colony at Matagorda had died and by early 1687, fewer than 45 people remained. Leaving a few colonists at the settlement, La Salle led 17 men, including his brother and two of his nephews, on a quest to French Illinois.

A few weeks later, some of the exhausted men **mutinied**, killing La Salle's nephews and two others. As La Salle approached the camp the next day to look for his nephews, he was led into an ambush and shot dead by mutineer, Pierre Duhaut.

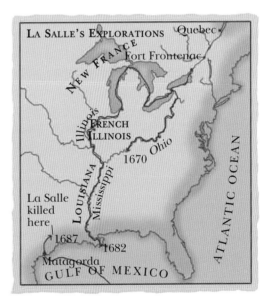

Fighting among the mutineers later led to the deaths of two other expedition members, including Pierre Duhaut. The remaining men made their way to Illinois and were finally rescued by Henri de Tonti's men. The Matagorda Bay colony lasted only until 1688, when natives killed nearly all of the settlers.

Grizzly Attack!

William Clark

The Lewis and Clark Expedition, known as the Corps of Discovery, was commissioned by American President Thomas Jefferson in 1803. Their mission was to explore the area contained within the **Louisiana Purchase**. The expedition would cross the western part of North America, starting near St. Louis on the Mississippi River, and heading westward all the way to the Pacific Ocean.

The Corps consisted of a group of U.S. Army volunteers under the command of Captain Meriwether Lewis and his close friend Second Lieutenant William Clark. They set off in May 1804, to explore and map the newly acquired territory, find a route across the western half of the continent, and establish a presence there before Britain and other European powers tried to claim the land.

The expedition faced many challenges, including stormy weather, first contact with many Native American tribes, and Spanish expeditions trying to stop their progress. The group hunted for much of their food. But one particular animal nearly put an end to Lewis. The expedition had come across grizzly bears before. Everyone knew that they were ferocious animals, especially when wounded. Once it had taken eight shots to kill a single grizzly. On June 14, Lewis was out hunting and had just shot a buffalo. As he waited for the animal to die, a grizzly appeared twenty paces away.

Meriwether Lewis

He raised his gun but realized too late it was not loaded. The bear was closing in on him fast, and he had no time to reload. The bear gave a roar and lumbered toward him. Lewis turned and ran for the river below. Just as the grizzly was almost upon him, he leaped into the river. When he was up to his waist, Lewis turned and pointed his unloaded **spontoon** at the bear. Luckily, the grizzly suddenly turned as if frightened and ran off.

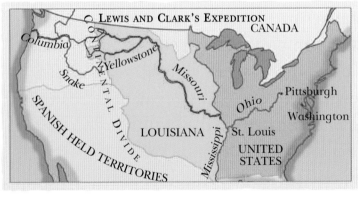

The expedition reached the Pacific coast in November 1805. Leaving the following March, the Corps returned to St. Louis by September 23, 1806. Mapping the area and establishing their presence gave the United States government a legal claim to the land. They also established trade with about 24 Native American nations.

Lion Attack!

It was David Livingstone's heartfelt mission to bring Christianity to the people of Africa that inspired his intrepid explorations of the African continent.

David Livingstone

In 1836, Livingstone began studying medicine and religion in Glasgow, Scotland. He decided to become a doctor. In 1841, he was sent as a **missionary** to the edge of the Kalahari Desert in southern Africa. One day, Livingstone was working on the ditches of a water channel when people began screaming for help from across the valley. A lion was dragging off some of the farmers' sheep. Livingstone immediately picked up his gun and ran to help. Seeing the lion, he fired both barrels of his shotgun but failed to kill the animal. He tried to reload but the lion was upon him in an instant. Grabbing him by the arm, it shook him viciously, making huge gashes in his flesh and splintering the bone.

A old man named Mebalwe arrived with a gun and fired at the animal, but the gun misfired. The noise attracted the lion who

then turned on Mebalwe. Suddenly the lion dropped dead, fatally wounded by Livingstone who had managed to reload. He and Mebalwe survived, but Livingstone's arm was permanently disabled.

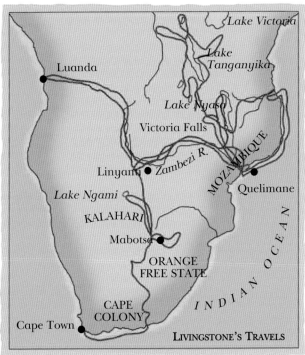

LIVINGSTONE'S TRAVELS

Livingstone later became famous for his five-year journey down the Zambezi River in southern Africa to its mouth in the Indian Ocean. Along the way he discovered a magnificent waterfall and named it Victoria Falls after Queen Victoria of England. Livingstone also searched unsuccessfully for the source of the Nile River in Egypt. Livingstone became a national hero in Britain and died in Africa in 1873 after suffering from poor health for years.

The Berbera Disaster

Richard Francis Burton

John Hanning Speke

Richard Burton was an officer in the British East India Company army and a renowned explorer. In 1854 he was preparing an expedition to explore deep inside Somaliland in Africa, and beyond. He was accompanied by Lieutenant John Speke, Lieutenant G. E. Herne, Lieutenant William Stroyan, and a number of Africans employed as **porters**. They were camped outside Berbera where a large fair was coming to a close.

On the morning of April 10, 1854, a band of 200 Somali warriors attacked the camp. As shots rang out, Speke bounced out of bed with his pistol in his hand. Running to Burton's tent, he found him loading his pistol. Burton called out to him, "Don't step back, or they'll think we are running."

Offended that Burton might be calling him a coward, Speke immediately ran forward, firing at the attackers. As more Somalis advanced on them, his pistol jammed and he was thrown to the ground by several men. At the same time, Stroyan was killed by a spear and Burton was seriously wounded by a spear, which pierced his cheeks. With the spear still lodged in his mouth, Burton managed to escape along with Herne. Speke was captured and his wrists were tied. One of the Somalis began to stab him, and Speke realized he would die if he did not do something quickly. He gave his tormentor a mighty blow to the head and ran for his life, dodging spears. He found Burton and Herne and the trio eventually managed to escape on a boat passing along the coast.

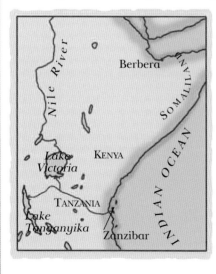

Two years later, Burton and Speke returned to explore Africa together and search for the source of the Nile River. They were the first Europeans to see lakes Tanganyika and Victoria despite being affected by severe illness and disease.

Nine Hours Too Late

Robert O'Hara Burke

The Victorian Exploring Expedition of 1860–61 (known as the Burke and Wills Expedition) was one of a number of teams racing to be first to cross the continent of Australia from the south. The center of the continent was unmapped and completely unknown.

The expedition set off from Melbourne on August 20, 1860. Nineteen men took 23 horses, six wagons, and 26 camels. Robert O'Hara Burke was the leader, although he had no experience in exploration or living in the bush. William John Wills was the **surveyor**, navigator, and third in command. Their heavily burdened wagons meant that they traveled slowly. By October 12, they had only reached Menindee, usually only a week's ride away.

Burke was aware that the experienced explorer, John McDouall Stuart, was competing for the prize for the first successful south-north crossing of the continent. Concerned that Stuart might beat him, Burke split up his group, taking seven of the fittest men and a small amount of equipment, planning to push on as quickly as possible to Coopers Creek, and then wait for the others to catch up. They arrived on November 11, but Burke decided to carry on rather than wait. He left William Brahe and three men at Coopers Creek with instructions to leave if Burke were not back in three months. Secretly, Wills told

Brahe to wait for four.

Burke, Wills, John King, and Charles Gray set off for the Gulf of Carpentaria on November 16. They had six camels, one horse, and enough food for just three months. They reached the gulf on February 9, 1861. They had only enough food left for 27 days on the return trip.

William John Wills

A tropical **monsoon** accompanied them on the trip back to Coopers Creek. Gray became ill and died of **dysentery**, and they had to shoot and eat three of their camels and a horse to survive. When they finally reached Coopers Creek on April 21, they found that Brahe and the others had left just nine hours earlier.

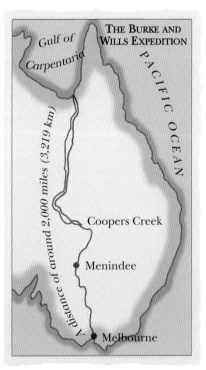

THE BURKE AND WILLS EXPEDITION

Gulf of Carpentaria

PACIFIC OCEAN

A distance of around 2,000 miles (3,219 km)

Coopers Creek

Menindee

Melbourne

The three men and two remaining camels were exhausted and had no hope of catching up to Brahe. Although supplies had been left for them at Coopers Creek, both Burke and Wills eventually died from starvation. King was found living with the Coopers Creek aborigines by a rescue team on September 15.

Lost in the Desert

Sven Hedin

Sven Hedin was a Swedish explorer who traveled through Asia and Europe between the late 1880s and early 1900s. During four expeditions to central Asia, he was the first European to see the Transhimalaya mountain range, Lake Lop Nur, and the Great Wall in China, and the first to discover the sources of the Brahmaputra, Indus, and Sutlej rivers in India. He also was first to see many ancient cities in the Taklamakan Desert in China. His expedition notes, precise mapping, and books about his travels filled in the uncharted areas of central Asia.

Although he was small and had a mild-mannered appearance, Hedin proved to be a determined explorer who survived many brushes with death. In 1895, on his first major expedition in central Asia to the Taklamakan Desert, Hedin's party ran out of water. The men resorted to drinking sheep's blood and camel's urine. The lack of water resulted in the deaths of two guides. A third member, Islam Bai, could not go on and was left at the campsite while Hedin traveled on with another guide, Kasim, to find water.

The two men ended up staggering and crawling across the desert, burying themselves in the sand to cool down and sucking moisture from the occasional plant they found. After a day and a night, Hedin came across tracks and realized with horror that the tracks were their own. They had traveled in a circle!

Kasim was too weak to continue, so Hedin set off on his own. He finally reached the banks of the river Khotan-Daria and drank his fill. He returned to Kasim with his waterproof boots full of water. Within hours they were picked up by a group of merchants who had also rescued Islam Bai.

Hedin had survived to continue his expedition, discovering the lost city of Dandan-Uiliq in China. He returned twice more to central Asia, mapping new areas that had been blank on European maps at that time.

Glossary

alliances Unions between different nations or armies

arqebus A firearm used from the 1400s to 1600s

basin An area of a river enclosed by land and deep enough for anchoring ships

causeway A raised road or railway, usually across a broad body of water

colony A territory, settled by people, which remains closely associated with the settlers' parent country

conquistadors The soldiers of the Spanish empire

dysentery An illness causing severe diarrhea

Louisiana Purchase The 530 million acres (2.14 million sq km) of territory in North America, bought by the United States from France in 1803

missionary A member of a religious group sent into an area to bring people to that religion

monsoon Very heavy rainfall

mutiny A rebellion against a leader

New World The Western Hemisphere, specifically the Americas

obsidian A dark glass formed by cooling lava

porter Someone that carries baggage for others

soldier of fortune A soldier who fights for money and adventure

spontoon A weapon like a spear, with two smaller blades on each side of the pointed blade

surveyor A person who evaluates and oversees lands

Index

Atahualpa 9
Aztec 6

Brahe, William 20, 21
Burke, Robert O'Hara 20, 21
Burton, Richard Francis 18

Cajamarca, Battle of 9
Champlain, Samuel de 10, 11
Clark, William 14, 15
Columbus, Christopher 5
Coopers Creek 20, 21
Cortés, Hernán 6, 8

Gray, Charles 21
Great Wall of China 22
Gulf of Carpentaria 21

Hedin, Sven 22
Herne, G. E. 18
Hormuz 5
Huron 10, 11

Inca Empire 8, 9
Indus River 22
Iroquois 10, 11

Kalahari Desert 16, 17
King, John 21
Kublai Khan 5

La Salle, Robert de 12, 13
Lake Lop Nur 22
Lake Tanganyika 17, 18
Lake Texcoco 6
Lake Victoria 17, 18
Lewis, Meriwether 14, 15

Livingstone, David 16, 17
Louisiana 12, 13, 14, 15

Matagorda Bay 13
Mississippi, River 12, 13, 14, 15
Moctezuma 6
Montenegro 8, 9

New France 10, 11, 12, 13
Nile, River 17, 18

Otumba, Battle of 6

Panama 8, 9
Pizarro, Francisco 8, 9
Polo, Marco 5
Punta Quemada, Battle of 8, 9

Quebec 10, 11, 13

Speke, John 18
Stroyan, William 18
Stuart, John McDouall 20

Taklamakan Desert 22
Tenochtitlan 6
Tonti, Henri de 12, 13

Victoria Falls 17, 18

Wills, William John 20, 21

Zambezi River 17